WOMEN WINNERS

THEN AND NOW

**By Lois Cantwell
and
Pohla Smith**

A SPORTS ILLUSTRATED FOR KIDS BOOK

Women Winners: Then and Now by Lois Cantwell and Pohla Smith

SPORTS ILLUSTRATED FOR KIDS and **KiDS** are registered trademarks of Time Inc.

Cover design and interior design by Emily Peterson Perez
Front-cover photographs by James Drake/Sports Illustrated (Lieberman-Cline);
Barry Gossage/WNBA Photos (Leslie); Bob Tringali/SportsChrome USA (Kwan);
John Zimmerman/Sports Illustrated (Fleming). Back-cover photographs: Henk
Koster/Newsport (Williams); Corbis-Bettman (Gibson)

Women Winners: Then and Now is published by SPORTS ILLUSTRATED FOR KIDS, a division of Time Inc. Its trademark is registered in the U.S. Patent and Trademark Office
and in other countries. SPORTS ILLUSTRATED FOR KIDS, 135 West 50th St., 4th Floor,
New York, N.Y. 10020-1393

For information, address: SPORTS ILLUSTRATED FOR KIDS

ISBN 1-930623-09-7
Printed in the United States of America

10 9 8 7 6 5 4 3 2 1

Women Winners: Then and Now is a production of SPORTS ILLUSTRATED
FOR KIDS Books: Cathrine Wolf, Assistant Managing Editor (project editor);
Emily Peterson Perez, Art Director; Margaret Sieck, Senior Editor;
Aaron Derr, Associate Editor; Kathleen Fieffe, Reporter; Robert J. Rohr, Copy
Manager; Erin Tricarico, Photo Researcher; Ron Beuzenburg, Production Manager

CONTENTS

For my daughter, Zoe Annie:
She runs, she jumps, she scores, and she talks on the phone, does her nails, and shops. The more things change, the more they stay the same! Title IX forever!
— Lois Cantwell

For all the women who made it possible for girls to play and work with the boys.
— Pohla Smith

INTRODUCTION

IMAGINE FOR A MINUTE THAT YOU HAVE MAGICALLY BEEN transported back to 1969. Look around: There's no cable TV, no personal computers, no microwaves. Cell phones, cordless phones, and answering machines don't exist. There are no CDs, VCRs, or DVDs. The internet? *Forget about it.*

People *are* excited about the prospect of man walking on the moon. *That* seems more likely than a woman receiving an athletic scholarship to college or pro teams for *girls*.

Three years later, that would begin to change after the U.S. Congress passed the 1972 Educational Amendments. One section of the law, Title IX, did away with discrimination in federally funded education programs, including athletics. Suddenly, schools *had* to provide equal sports facilities and teams for boys and girls. Girls were given a chance to run, jump, play ball, and skate as never before.

Lisa Leslie, Venus Williams, and Marion Jones are just a few of the millions of young girls who grew up after Title IX, proud of their sports skills. Compare their stories with the athletes who were trailblazers, brave women like Althea Gibson and Janet Guthrie, who succeeded despite the odds.

Read the stories in *Women Winners: Then and Now* and be inspired. Shoot some hoops or challenge your friends to a race. Strive to always do your best, and you'll be a winner, too!

HOOPS

NANCY LIEBERMAN-CLINE
AND
LISA LESLIE

If Nancy Lieberman and Lisa Leslie had been in the same class, they probably would have challenged each other to daily games of one-on-one. But they were born almost 20 years apart. What a difference that time made! As a teen, Nancy roamed around looking for pickup games; Lisa was wildly cheered on in her high school gym.

Title IX is the genie that let girls' sports dreams come true.

NANCY LIEBERMAN-CLINE

IT HAD TO BE A PASSING FAD.

After all, it was the 1970's. Most girls growing up in Far Rockaway, New York, at the time wanted to go shopping or talk on the telephone or hang out with their best friends.

Not Nancy Lieberman. She *loved* playing football. When her mother, Renee Lieberman, looked out the window, she often saw a pile of bodies in the backyard. But she couldn't see Nancy. Why? Because she was at the bottom of the pile!

Finally, Nancy's mom put her foot down and insisted that Nancy stop playing football with the neighborhood boys. So, Nancy took up basketball instead. The rest, as the saying goes, is history. That redheaded "tomboy" grew up to be Nancy Lieberman-Cline, one of the best women basketball players ever!

LOOKING FOR A GAME

Nancy was born on July 1, 1958, in Brooklyn, New York. Despite what some people think, she was *not* born with a basketball in her hand, and she didn't take her first steps while dribbling a basketball. But she did like sports early on.

When Nancy was a baby, her family moved to Far Rockaway, Queens, another part of New York City. Her parents divorced when she was 12. After that Nancy and her older brother, Cliff, were brought up by their mother. Cliff was an excellent student. Nancy put all her energy into sports.

Life was not easy for female athletes then. Title IX, which makes sure that schools and colleges give girls the same opportunity to play sports as boys, was not yet law. There were few organized teams for girls, and Nancy was not allowed to play in the boys' public-school leagues. Instead, she played whenever and wherever she could.

Nancy's nickname was "Fire" because of her bright red hair. The nickname also fit because she had a *burning* desire to compete. She started going beyond the neighborhood to play basketball. She rode the subway to Harlem, in a distant part of New York City, looking for the perfect game. As a high school junior, she played for the New York Chuckles, a boys' Amateur Athletic Union team, in Harlem.

JAMES DRAKE/SPORTS ILLUSTRATED

Playing against boys helped Nancy keep a step ahead of most female opponents.

Nancy was different, but she didn't care. Her mother, though, was concerned about Nancy's future. At the time, women's pro sports were just a daydream. Nancy's mom said a career as a nurse or secretary would be better. But Nancy stood firm, even after her mom punctured her basketball with a screwdriver to stop her non-stop playing!

Many schools didn't have girls' basketball teams then. When girls played, they wore skirts or jumpers. There was a special set of rules for girls, too. For example, a player could dribble for no more than three bounces before passing or shooting.

That was not the game Nancy played. At the beach near her home or on city courts, she played with boys and learned the "boys" game. She picked up outstanding passing, shooting, and scrambling skills. At night, she played "radar ball" games on courts lit only by dim streetlights.

That helped her develop a better touch. When the weather was too lousy to play outdoors, Nancy practiced indoors. She drove her mother crazy getting finger marks on the ceiling as she practiced jumping. She grew to 5'10" and learned to throw blind passes, one-handers, and other flashy dishes.

People began to notice Nancy. In 1973, at age 15, she was named one of the 12 members of the U.S. National Team. In 1976, at the Montreal (Canada) Olympics, she became the youngest U.S. basketball player ever to win a silver medal.

SCHOOL DAZE

After the Olympics, Nancy entered Old Dominion University, in Norfolk, Virginia. Title IX had been passed and ODU took women's sports seriously. It had fine facilities and coaches. It was the first school in Virginia to give athletic scholarships to women, and Nancy was the first woman!

Playing forward and point guard, Nancy averaged 18.1 points, 8.3 rebounds, and 7.2 assists per game in her four seasons at ODU. She had more than 700 steals and led the team to back-to-back national college championships. She collected awards galore and a new nickname: Lady Magic, after Earvin "Magic" Johnson, the slick-passing star who led Michigan State University to the 1979 men's national college championship. Later, he became an NBA All-Star.

Nancy graduated from ODU in 1980. She hoped to go to the Olympics, in Moscow, in the Soviet Union. But the U.S. boycotted the Games for political reasons.

So, Nancy found another game. In 1981, the Women's Basketball League (WBL) was formed. The Dallas Diamonds named Nancy their top draft pick. The WBL had trouble attracting fans and TV coverage, and folded after the season — after Nancy led Dallas to the championship series.

Nancy became a personal trainer for tennis pro Martina Navratilova, and did some broadcasting and newspaper writing. When the Women's American Basketball Association (WABA) was formed, in 1984, Nancy signed with another pro team, also called the Dallas Diamonds. But that league lasted just one season as well.

PLAYING THE BOYS, AGAIN

Then, in 1986, Nancy scored a major sports first: She became the first woman to play for a *men's* pro team! She played point guard for the Springfield Fame of the U.S. Basketball League (USBL), a minor league of former college stars. She played for the Long Island Knights in 1987. In two USBL seasons, Nancy played 40 games and had 59 assists, 50 points, 22 rebounds, and 13 steals. Later, she joined the Washington Generals, the team that travels and plays the Harlem Globetrotters, and met her husband, Tim Cline.

When the WNBA began, in 1997, Nancy thought of making a comeback as a player, at age 39! Instead, she found another way to be a part of the game. In 1998, she was named the general manager/head coach of the Detroit Shock.

Nancy had finally found a league of her own.

LISA LESLIE

LISA LESLIE WAS BORN ON JULY 7, 1972, EXACTLY TWO WEEKS after President Richard Nixon signed Title IX into law. Talk about good timing! If Lisa had been born 20 years earlier, she would never have become the international basketball star that she is — no matter how much talent she had. Back then, there was no pro league or Olympic basketball for women. College athletic scholarships were rarely offered to girls.

Lisa came along as things were changing, and she had the talent and desire to take advantage of those changes. She became the star center of the WNBA's Los Angeles Sparks and a key member of two gold-medal U.S. Olympic basketball teams.

Off the basketball court, Lisa made a name for herself, too. She is a fashion model and has appeared in magazines such as *Vogue* and *Shape*. Lisa has stunning looks. The fact that athletic women were accepted more in the 1990's than they had been a generation earlier helped her. "Most of the companies that hire me like my athletic look," Lisa said.

LONG, TALL, LITTLE LISA

Lisa's parents were both tall, and so was Lisa. Her mother, Christine, is 6' 3" tall and her father, Walter, was 6' 4". When Lisa was in third grade, she was taller than her teacher. By the sixth grade, she had reached six feet! Lisa's height made her feel self-conscious sometimes. "I was teased because I was tall and thin," Lisa recalled. "Kids called me Olive Oyl."

Lisa thought her mother was the most beautiful woman in the world. She wanted people to say *she* was pretty and elegant, too, like her mom. Lisa's mom would have her and her sister Tiffany walk around the house balancing books on their head in an effort to teach them to walk more smoothly.

Lisa wanted people to see more than her height. But that was difficult, especially after Lisa started playing sports. Her athletic career took off in a *dramatic* way when she was at Morningside High School, in Inglewood, California. In a school play, Lisa had the role of Wilma Rudolph, a track star at the 1960 Olympics. Lisa had to run quickly around the auditorium. She ran so fast that the track coach came to see her. On the spot, he asked her to join the track team!

CENTER OF ATTENTION

Lisa also played volleyball and basketball. She earned some national publicity in 1990 when she scored 101 points during the first *half* of a Morningside basketball game. The other team was so embarrassed that it wouldn't come out for the second half! At that time, the most points ever scored by an individual in a girls' high school basketball game was 105. Lisa didn't get to break that record but she received a lot of attention.

Lisa received attention for other things, too. "As a high school athlete, I was put down for wearing makeup," she said. "I was accused of trying to be cute instead of playing seriously. But on the court I got the job done. My hair was neat, my nails were polished, and I wore lipstick when I played. I think it's cool to be feminine on the court. You can't judge people by how they look."

Colleges judged Lisa by how she *played*, and they were impressed. Lisa accepted a scholarship to the University of Southern California (USC). That way she was able to stay close to home, and her family could come to cheer her on.

They had a lot to cheer about. Lisa averaged more than 20 points per game over her USC career. By the time she was done, Lisa had scored 2,414 points — more than any other female in the history of the Pacific 10 Conference. Lisa had also broken Pacific 10 records for rebounds and blocked shots, and been named the National Player of the Year.

After college, in 1994, Lisa wanted to keep playing. Since there was no professional league for women in the U.S., Lisa did what many top players did: She went to Europe.

MATT YORK/AP

Playing for her hometown team, Lisa became one of the first WNBA stars.

She joined a pro team in Alcamo, Italy, and averaged 22.6 points and 11.7 rebounds. She also learned how to be more aggressive on the court.

But for Lisa, there was no place like home. After one season in Italy, Lisa was recruited to play for the U.S. national team. The squad traveled all over the world, playing games against college and national teams, to prepare for the 1996 Olympics. At the Games, in Atlanta, the team easily won the gold medal. Lisa scored 29 points in the championship game to help the U.S. defeat world champion Brazil. For the tournament, she led the team in scoring — just as she would again four years later when she led the U.S. to another gold medal, at the 2000 Olympics, in Sydney, Australia.

MODEL PLAYER

In 1996, Lisa signed a contract with Wilhelmina Models, an agency that helps people find jobs appearing in advertisements and fashion magazines. Lisa modeled evening gowns in *Shape* magazine and sports gear in *Vogue* and *TV Guide*.

Finally, in 1997, the Women's National Basketball Association (WNBA) was established. For Lisa, and other American women, that meant a chance to play professionally without going overseas. Lisa was one of the first players signed to a WNBA contract. She was excited when she got to play for her new hometown team, the Los Angeles Sparks. She worked hard in practice and was one of the league's best players from day one.

When the WNBA held its first All-Star Game, in 1999, Lisa scored 13 points and grabbed five rebounds to win the MVP award. Through her first four WNBA seasons, Lisa averaged more than 17 points and nine rebounds per game. The Sparks twice advanced to the Western Conference Finals but were defeated both times by the Houston Comets. That was nothing to be embarrassed about: The Comets won the first *four* WNBA championships!

Some of the biggest stars in the NBA were impressed with Lisa's play. "Lisa is versatile," said super guard Kobe Bryant of the Los Angeles Lakers. "She's tall, but she's still athletic and mobile. And she has a soft shooting touch."

Added Seattle SuperSonic forward Vin Baker: "Lisa can shoot the jumper or play with her back to the basket. She's a good rebounder. She's a smooth player."

She even had a basketball shoe named after her, an honor few athletes receive. Nike designed a shoe called "Total Air 9," after Lisa's number.

In addition to basketball and modeling, Lisa works as a broadcaster and does charity work. In 1999, she received the Young Heroes Award from the Big Sisters Guild of Los Angeles for her work with foster children. Lisa leads a busy life, but she makes the moves from one job to another as smoothly as she moves on the basketball court.

CARS

JANET GUTHRIE AND SARAH FISHER

A race car is a machine. It doesn't know if its driver is male or female, young or old. All that matters is whether the driver can get the most out of the machine. Unfortunately, car owners and racing fans know the difference, and the sport remained a men's club for many years.

These two women, Janet Guthrie and Sarah Fisher, love to go fast. Read how they tried — or are trying — not to let attitudes or anything else slow them down.

JANET GUTHRIE

YOU DON'T HAVE TO KNOW MUCH ABOUT AUTO RACING TO know about the Indianapolis 500. Held in late May, the Indy 500 is an American tradition. Until the early 1970's, it was an *all-male* American tradition. No women were allowed in "Gasoline Alley," where the cars are serviced. No female drivers ever entered the race. That's the way it had always been. That is, until Janet Guthrie came along.

Janet was born in Iowa City, Iowa, in 1938. At the time, girls and boys acted and were treated very differently. Janet

Fantastic first: In 1977, Janet became the first woman to compete in the famous Indianapolis 500.

didn't fit the "girl" mold of the time. Girls were supposed to play jump-rope, hold tea parties, and wear nice dresses. Boys climbed trees, built soapbox racers, and muddied their jeans.

But Janet liked adventure, and she didn't care much if it was the kind of activity girls were "supposed to do" or not.

Janet is the oldest of five children (three girls, two boys). Her father, William, was an airline pilot and her mother, Jean Ruth, was a stay-at-home mom. The family moved quite a bit before settling in Miami, Florida.

As a youngster, Janet was attracted to anything that traveled *fast*. She began flying lessons at age 13. When she was 16 years old, she wanted to try parachute jumping. Her parents weren't too sure about that idea! But sometime after Janet jumped from the roof of her one-story home to prove that she could handle the landing roll, they finally agreed to let her leap from a plane. Janet made a perfect landing.

Janet wasn't like most of the girls attending Miss Harris's Florida School for Girls in the 1950's. Many of them shied away from studying math and science. They did not fly planes or race cars much, either. Janet did all those things. After graduating, she went to the University of Michigan to study physics. Then she took a job in the aerospace division of Republic Aviation, on Long Island, New York. It was the 1960's and space exploration was on the way. Janet helped develop some of the stress tests that NASA gave astronauts before sending them into space.

RACING TAKES OVER

Janet needed a car to get to work, and she decided to buy the most beautiful car she knew, a Jaguar XK-120. Then she wanted to see how it handled at top speed. Before long, she joined a car club that sponsored races, called gymkhanas. They were tests of skill, reflexes, and speed. Janet became the undisputed women's champ of Long Island.

Between 1960 and 1965, Janet worked and raced. What drew her to racing? Janet has said that love of racing came slowly to her. Unlike Sarah Fisher *(see page 21)*, racing was not a goal she had been aiming toward her whole life. But being behind the wheel felt as natural and comfortable to Janet as breathing. So she decided to do more of it.

Janet enrolled at a racing school in Lime Rock, Connecticut. She started competing in regular stock-car races, such as the Watkins Glen 500, Sebring 12-hour, and Daytona 24-hour endurance races. She completed nine consecutive races at one point.

Janet's career in physics began to take a backseat to her racing career. During the early 1970's, she worked as a technical writer, but she also tried to race full-time. She had no backers or financial support. She did her own mechanical work and sent out letters asking for support.

Unfortunately, although Janet was ready for professional racing, it wasn't ready for her. By 1975, her racing career was going nowhere. Then, suddenly, things changed. Indy race-car owner Rolla Vollstedt was looking for a driver. He hired Janet. It was just the break she needed. Indy-car racing was the *biggest* of big-time racing in the U.S. Janet was to be a part of it!

MOVE OVER, FELLOWS

Janet made her Indy 500 circuit debut at the U.S. Auto Club event at Trenton (New Jersey) International Speedway. She was not prepared for the commotion caused by her appearance. A lot of people were upset. Some claimed that a woman in the race would *endanger* the lives of the men because, they said, women were bad drivers!

Most of the male drivers hated the idea of a female racer. One of them boasted that he could pick up a hitchhiker, teach him how to drive, and make him a better driver than Janet was. The remarks were cruel, but Janet pressed on. Between

1976 and 1980, she competed in 33 Indy races, finished in the Top 10 five times, and earned $58,792.

Car trouble kept Janet out of the 1976 Indy 500, but in 1977, she qualified for the most famous race in the country. Whether they liked it or not, race officials, drivers, and fans all knew Janet was making history when the starter of the race said: "Gentlemen, in the company of the first lady ever to start the Indianapolis 500, start your engines."

It wasn't a good race for Janet. Her fuel tank flooded, drenching her with gasoline, which burned and blistered her skin. Then her car gave out completely.

In 1978, Janet again qualified for the Indy 500. She started in 15th place and finished in ninth — ahead of 24 other cars — all driven by men! Janet earned her biggest paycheck, $24,115, for that finish. The next year, Janet started at Indy again, qualifying in 14th place and finishing 34th. She and Rolla Vollstedt parted ways after that. Janet couldn't find a new sponsor and, in 1980, she retired from auto racing.

Courage is a great quality. So is determination. Janet had both in abundance. She refused to be told no just because she was a female. Instead, she pursued her passions with vigor. She knocked down barriers and opened the door for other female drivers.

That's why, even though she never collected the pile of victories some athletes do, Janet *was* a winner.

SARAH FISHER

IN SPRING OF 1999, RACE-CAR DRIVER Sarah Fisher visited an elementary school near Indianapolis, Indiana. She was there to read to the young students, and she chose one of her favorite books called *The Little Engine That Could*, by Watty Piper. It was an appropriate choice. Like the Little Engine That Could, Sarah has always believed in herself, set goals, and then worked toward them.

And, like the Little Engine, Sarah has had a *good* ride.

In 2000, Sarah became the third — and youngest — woman ever to compete in the Indy 500. She was only 19.

BORN TO RACE

Sarah was born on October 4, 1980, in Commercial Point, Ohio. It was a time when gender barriers in the sports world were quickly coming down. She didn't have to put up with many of the attitudes that Janet Guthrie had faced for participating in "boys activities." Auto racing, especially,

In 2000, Sarah became the youngest woman to compete at Indy.

was not an issue. Sarah's mother, Reba, was a middle-school teacher. Her father, Dave, owned a machinery shop. But Mr. and Mrs. Fisher had met and fallen in love racing go-carts.

By the time Sarah was 5, she too wanted to race. She began in a quarter midget, which is a small version of a race car. She was racing open-form go-karts at age 8, sprint cars at 15, and full midgets at 17.

"Your family tries to involve you in similar interests," Sarah said. "If your parents play basketball, they'll try to get you to play basketball. I enjoyed racing so much I took it as a great hobby, and [then tried] to look at it as a career."

When Sarah began racing, her parents served as her coaches and crew. At 11, she won the World Karting Association (WKA) grand national championship in the 125-cc engine class. After she won two more WKA titles, it was clear that Sarah was serious about racing.

Like most individuals who reach the top of their profession, Sarah had to make sacrifices to be successful. In her case, that meant missing out on a lot of typical high school activities. She attended only one football game and only one basketball game in four years at Teays (Ohio) High School. She was *too* busy. If she wasn't racing or practicing, she was studying. She graduated in 1999 with an A average. "I wasn't very popular," Sarah said. "I was different. What other kid takes racing as a career when they are that young? Let's face it. I'm not the average go-to-the-prom girl."

After high school, Sarah put college on hold for a year so

that she could concentrate on racing. In 2000, she entered Butler University, in Indianapolis, Indiana.

"I just want to get a college degree," Sarah said. "In racing, you've always got to have a Plan B in case something happens. But Plan A is most important."

STICKING WITH PLAN A

Plan A is Sarah's racing career. In August 1999, she qualified for the Indy Racing League (IRL). By October, she was racing, at the Mall.com 500 in Texas. She began to work with a professional pit crew.

In her first race, Sarah finished 17th out of 27. That performance impressed owner Derrick Walker, who was looking for a rookie to join his team. He chose Sarah.

In May 2000, Sarah qualified for the Indy 500 with an average speed of 220 miles per hour. That earned her a starting spot in the *second* row. On May 28, two women started in the Indy 500 for the first time, Sarah and Lyn St. James. Unfortunately, Sarah and Lyn, in her second Indy 500, collided early in the race. Both drivers lost control, hit the restraining wall, and had to drop out. Neither was injured.

In August, Sarah finished third in the Kentucky Speedway Open, just 7.749 seconds out of second place. That was the highest finish ever by a woman in Indy racing.

That fantastic *finish* might have have been the *start* of something big for Sarah. ♕

RACKETS

ALTHEA GIBSON AND VENUS WILLIAMS

*I*n July 2000, Venus Williams became only the second African-American woman to win the most famous tournament in all of tennis, the All England Championship at Wimbledon. Althea Gibson was the first, having taken the championship more than 40 years earlier.

Not too much else, however, is similar about the stories of these two remarkable athletes.

ALTHEA GIBSON

IF ALTHEA GIBSON'S LIFE STORY WERE MADE INTO A TV movie, the director would want to change the ending. The story starts off somewhat like Cinderella's, with Althea rising above a rough, poor childhood and the twin obstacles of sexism and racism to become the queen of tennis.

Except Althea didn't wind up in a fairy-tale castle for the rest of her life.

Althea Gibson was born on August 25, 1927, in Silver, South Carolina. Her family were sharecroppers. Sharecroppers farm land that belongs to someone else. They work hard but only share a part of the crops they raise; the landowner gets the rest. It is a very poor existence.

Daniel and Annie Gibson wanted a better life for their five children. They moved the family to Harlem, in New York City.

Althea was a curious child. "I was mischievous," she said. "I got into things a lot." In elementary school, she got into a bad habit. Instead of going to class, she roamed the neighborhood, checking things out. She felt she was learning about life.

School officials, of course, wanted her to do her learning in the classroom. They reported her for playing hooky. When Althea's father was told, he would lose his temper and beat her. But Althea kept on.

One summer day, while exploring the area, Althea saw kids playing sports on

Althea played a quick, athletic style that had never before been seen in women's tennis.

CORBIS-BETTMAN

25

streets that had been closed to traffic. It was the New York Police Athletic League's "play street" recreation program. Althea was delighted to join in. She loved basketball and was a good athlete. That's where Althea first held a racket. She took up paddle tennis, which is played with a wood paddle and a rubber ball. Soon, Althea was the paddle-tennis champion of the city!

CLOSED COURTS

When Althea was 13, the director of New York's Police Athletic League, Buddy Walker, saw her playing paddle tennis. He figured if Althea was good with a paddle, she might be great with a racket. He introduced her to the game of tennis and to her first coach, Fred Johnson.

By 1944, Althea had won the American Tennis Association (ATA) junior national championship. The ATA was a tennis organization especially for African Americans. Two African-American doctors, Hubert Eaton and Walter Johnson, saw how much talent Althea had. They thought she might be able to break the sport's color line.

In the 1940's, black and white Americans went to separate schools, ate in separate restaurants, and stayed at separate hotels in most parts of the country. In tennis, it was unheard of for black players to join a white-only club or even be invited to play on the courts.

The U.S. Lawn Tennis Association, which governed the sport, had rules that forbade discrimination. But neither the USLTA nor other major tournament organizers invited black players to play. That's why the ATA had been formed.

Dr. Johnson and Dr. Eaton took Althea into their homes, so that she could work on her tennis and finish high school. She attended Williston High School, in Wilmington, North Carolina. Meadowlark Lemon, who grew up to be a Harlem Globetrotter, was a student there.

"I used to sit down and watch her," Meadowlark later recalled. "Man, she was an athlete. I saw her play softball, basketball, touch football, everything. That lady did it all."

Mostly, though, Althea did tennis. She was an enormously gifted player. Other players on nearby courts would stop their games to watch her play. She was *that* good.

By the late 1940's, Althea was ranked Number 1 in the ATA. She wanted to play with the best *white* players. At age 23, she finally got that chance.

Alice Marble, a four-time U.S. Open champion, wrote a letter to the USLTA's magazine. She said she was embarrassed Althea was not allowed to play in their tournaments.

BREAKING BARRIERS

Almost immediately, Althea was invited to play in the USLTA National Championship (now the U.S. Open). In 1950, she became the first black player to play — and win — a match in that important tournament. Althea endured terrible racial insults and taunts. She answered them with talent. At 5' 11", she had a reach advantage over opponents.

She was strong, and she played a quick, aggressive game never before seen in women's tennis.

In 1956, Althea won the French Open and became the first black player to win a Grand Slam championship. In the next two years, she won four more Slam events — including Wimbledon and the U.S. Nationals twice each — and was ranked the Number 1 female tennis player in the world.

All told, Althea won 11 Grand Slam singles and doubles championships. She might have won more, but she couldn't earn enough money to support herself by playing tennis, so she retired in 1958.

She found other ways to make a living. She had a wonderful voice and recorded an album, "Althea Gibson Sings." She went on the "Ed Sullivan Show" on TV and appeared in a movie. In 1960, she toured with the Harlem Globetrotters, giving exhibition tennis matches before their games.

Althea took up golf and, in 1963, at the age of 35, she broke another barrier by becoming the first black woman to join the Ladies Professional Golf Association tour. In 1975, she was named the New Jersey State Athletic Commissioner. She also headed the recreation program in East Orange, New Jersey. That was another first.

In 2000, when Venus Williams won Wimbledon, Althea was in poor health and living alone in East Orange. The woman who had been called the "Jackie Robinson of tennis" was not rich and famous. She was all but forgotten.

VENUS WILLIAMS

IN THE LATE 1800'S, TENNIS WAS A GENTEEL GAME. RICH society people played it on grass courts at private clubs or mansions. Tennis clothes were all white and so, for the most part, were the players.

The style of play was mannerly, too, especially among the women. They were more or less covered from head to toe in bulky skirts and matching hats. Running and diving for a ball was considered unladylike, not to mention nearly impossible!

Fast-forward a century, or so, to the late 1980's and check out the tennis being played in Compton, California: Two young black girls dodging and darting all over cracked, trash-covered tennis courts in a public park. They're learning the game not from a fancy pro, but from their dad, who picked up most of what he knows by reading books and watching videos. Nearby, drug dealers do business and sometimes gun shots from a drive-by shooting echo through the streets.

Those girls are Venus and Serena Williams. By

Venus rising: Victories at Wimbledon and the U.S. Open in 2000 proved that Venus had arrived.

the end of the century, they would become two of the best, and most revolutionary, tennis players ever. In 2000, Venus matched Althea Gibson's feat of winning Wimbledon and the U.S. Open. She became the first African-American woman in 42 years to win Wimbledon, and only the second African American — male or female — to win two Grand Slam events in the same year. What a difference a century makes!

STARTING YOUNG

Venus Ebone Starr Williams was born on June 17, 1980, the fourth of five daughters. Serena, her tennis partner and challenger, is the baby of the Williams family. Venus's mother, Oracene, is called Brandi. Venus's father, Richard, came from a family of sharecroppers.

One day, after the first three Williams girls were born, Mr. Williams happened to see a tennis match on TV. He decided right then and there that his next two children would learn to play tennis.

From the time they were about 5 years old, Venus and Serena practiced and practiced. When Venus was 11, the family moved to Palm Beach Gardens, Florida, so that she and Serena could train with a tennis pro named Rick Macci. At 14, Venus became a professional tennis player.

Tennis was a huge part of Venus's life, but it was not her *entire* life. After moving to Florida, she attended school in Delray Beach for a while, then she was home-schooled for a while. For fun, she and Serena surfed and rode jet-skis. Venus speaks several languages, and has dreamed of becoming — in no particular order — an astronaut, a TV personality, an architect, a fashion designer, and a paleontologist (a person who studies prehistoric plants and animals).

In January 1998, Venus graduated from high school, with a B+ average. By then her tennis career had started to soar. She began the year 1997 ranked 211th in the world, and she ended it ranked 64th! At the U.S. Open, she stunned opponents — and tennis fans — and reached the final, before losing to Martina Hingis.

In 1998, Venus became the only unseeded player to reach the quarterfinals of the Australian Open and won her first pro singles title, the IGA Tennis Classic. She was 17.

SISTER, SISTER

Both will *and* sisterly love were tested in 1999. Serena and Venus are best friends. They are also very competitive, so they avoid playing against each other by playing different tournaments. Still, Venus *is* the older sister. But it was Serena who beat Martina, 6–3, 7–6, at the 1999 U.S. Open to become the first Williams to win a Grand Slam title. (Venus had lost to Martina Hingis in a tough match the day before.)

A few weeks later, Serena beat Venus for the first time. Then painful tendinitis in her wrists knocked Venus out of tennis completely for a while. There was talk of her retiring.

Yeah, right! Venus came back strong in the spring of 2000. She faced Serena in a semi-final match at Wimbledon.

Venus triumphed, 6–2, 7–6, winning the tiebreaker 7–3. She beat Lindsay Davenport, 6–3, 7–6, (7–3 in the tiebreaker), and Venus had her Grand Slam title. She was ready: Venus had already bought a gown for the Champions' Ball! She had bought it after losing in the quarterfinals of the 2000 French Open. *That's* how sure of herself Venus can be.

While she was playing those final Wimbledon matches, Venus thought about Althea Gibson. "I knew she was watching [last year] when Serena won the U.S. Open," Venus said. "She said that she was happy she got to see another black person win it in her lifetime. So now I think it's really a privilege for me to win this Wimbledon while she's still alive."

GOOD AND GOLD

For the first time, sisters had won Grand Slam championships. Two months later, when Venus won the 2000 U.S. Open, sisters had won back-to-back U.S. Opens for the first time. Looking at her name on the U.S. Open Cup, Venus said, "It feels really nice because it's right next to Serena's name."

Venus's awesome year continued at the 2000 Summer Olympics, in Sydney, Australia. There she won the gold medal for the singles competition, then teamed with Serena to win the gold in doubles. The 6–1, 6–1 victory over Kristie Boogert and Miriam Oremans of the Netherlands marked the 22nd straight win for the Williams sisters and has been called the most one-sided women's final in Olympic history.

Oh, sister!

BLADES

PEGGY FLEMING
AND
MICHELLE KWAN

igure skating is a sport in which women were always accepted. On skates, a woman can be feminine and athletic at the same time. No skaters have combined those attributes better than Peggy Fleming and Michelle Kwan. They make their jumps and spins look effortless. But don't be fooled: Both had to be tough as nails to succeed.

PEGGY FLEMING

PEGGY FLEMING BECAME A FIGURE SKATER PURELY BY CHANCE. When she was 9 years old, Peggy and her three sisters found themselves at an ice rink in Cleveland, Ohio. They decided to give skating a try. Peggy glided over the ice like a fish through water. "It was amazing," her sister Janice remembered. "She didn't wobble or anything; she just started skating as if she'd been at it for a long time."

Naturally, Peggy went on to become one of the best and most popular figure skaters ever. There may have been skating champions who did more athletic jumps since Peggy, but none that has been more graceful on the ice.

Becoming a champion wasn't as easy as learning to skate.

Her family moved often, and Peggy kept changing coaches. Skating was expensive. Peggy's dad, Albert, didn't make much money. But Peggy so clearly had talent that all the family made sacrifices to pay for her lessons and travel. Her dad took a second job. Her mom, Doris, made her skating dresses. Her sisters took on some of their parents' chores.

When Peggy finally got settled with a coach she liked, a terrible thing happened. In 1961, the plane that was carrying Peggy's coach, William Kipp, and all of the top U.S. coaches and skaters to a competition in Czechoslovakia, crashed! Everyone on the plane died.

For Peggy, it meant that, at age 12, she had no coach and no U.S. skating role models to follow. It also meant that U.S. skating needed new stars. Peggy moved up quickly through the ranks. In 1964, she won her first U.S. title and earned a trip to the Olympics. She finished sixth!

TRAGEDY STRIKES

Difficulty struck again that spring. While Peggy was touring Europe, her dad had a heart attack. Peggy wanted to quit skating to save the money while her father recovered. Her family wouldn't let her! Instead, they supported her even more, moving from California to Colorado Springs, Colorado, in 1965, so that she could train with the famous Carlo Fassi, who had come to the U.S. from Italy.

In 1966, Peggy won her third U.S. title. At the world championships, she upset the defending champion, Petra

Burka. Then Peggy's dad had another heart attack and died. Again, Peggy said that she would quit skating. Her family said no. "I want Peggy to win an Olympic gold medal," said sister Maureen.

At the 1968 Winter Games, Peggy did just that. The competition consisted of the free skate and "figures," in which skaters traced figure 8's into the ice. Peggy was good at the precise figures *and* at the creative free skating. She took a big lead in the figures.

At the 1968 Olympics, Peggy shone in the free skate and the figures.

AP

The next night, Peggy was terrific in the free skate, wearing the chartreuse-colored chiffon skating outfit her mom had made. When she was done skating, though, Peggy cried. She felt she had not skated well and had let people down. She was wrong: All nine judges placed Peggy first!

Peggy retired from amateur skating and turned pro later that year. She became a symbol of grace and beauty in athletics and gave many girls a role model at a time when there weren't many athletic women to look up too. ♕

MICHELLE KWAN

Thanks to Title IX, many girls and women were playing many different sports by the time Michelle Kwan was born on July 7, 1980. Is that what inspired her to become an athlete? No. She tried skating because her older brother played hockey! When Michelle was 5, her parents took her and her sister, Karen, to watch their brother, Ron, practice. Michelle and Karen wanted to skate, too. They liked it!

Two years later, Michelle won her first competition. At 13, she was the alternate to the U.S. women's Olympic team that went to Lillehammer, Norway. Two years after *that* she was the world champion! At 15, Michelle was one of the youngest world champions in figure-skating history.

Michelle became the most popular and best-known amateur skater in the nation, maybe even in the world. Like Peggy Fleming, Michelle made her mark with artistry and grace. Sure, she can do jumps and spins with the best of them, but what sets her apart is her artistic beauty. She is one of the most artistic amateur skaters since Peggy.

There's only one honor that escaped Michelle in the 20th century: an Olympic gold medal. She was the favorite to win at the 1998 Winter Games, in Nagano, Japan. But she did not skate her best in the free skate. She ended up second to 15-year-old Tara Lipinski, and took home a silver medal.

Michelle didn't give up. She decided to remain an amateur, keep training, and keep winning titles. She began to prepare for the 2002 Winter Olympics, in Salt Lake City, Utah.

Michelle simply loves skating and the challenge of trying to be perfect. "I want to be [in Salt Lake City] with all my heart, but I don't think that's why I'm doing this," she said. "It's more for the everyday challenge of skating, of competing, of trying to figure out why, if I've done that triple a million times in practice, I can miss it in competition."

After the Olympic disappointment, Michelle took a different approach to skating and her life. She had never gone to high school because she was training so hard. To earn her high school diploma, she studied with tutors. Michelle decided she needed more balance in her life. She wanted to prepare for a future off the ice, *and* she thought she might feel less pressure at skating competitions if she had other things to think about.

"I don't think life is about sticking to one thing," she told a Los Angeles paper. "It's about developing an all-around presence."

In Fall 1999, she entered college, at the University of California at Los Angeles

Michelle is the most graceful, artistic skater since Peggy Fleming, who was the 1968 Olympic champion.

PHIL COLE/ALLSPORT

(UCLA). She lived in a dormitory and went to classes, just as all students do. But she still woke up very early to skate, and spent many weekends traveling to competitions.

Finding the right balance between studies and skating was a challenge for Michelle. Her skating suffered during the first semester. She felt that she took too many classes, so she cut back during her second semester. The new routine worked. Michelle won her fourth U.S. championship and third world title that semester!

A SENIOR AT AGE 12

Being a full-time student and a world-class athlete is a big challenge, but Michelle has always pushed herself. When she was 11, she and her coach, Frank Carroll, disagreed on whether she should take the test to move up from junior competition to senior. Coach Carroll thought she should wait a year. Michelle waited only until he went away for a weekend! In May 1992, she took the test. She passed.

Coach Carroll told her, "Okay, we're going to have to work our butts off because you are going to make a dismal showing unless you develop some maturity and presence."

No problem. Michelle was used to such pronouncements. Her father, Danny, always told her that she had to work hard at skating if he was going to pay for such an expensive sport. She showed her dad and her coach that she was up to the challenge. At age 12, she went to the 1993 U.S. Olympic Festival, and won the gold medal! She also placed sixth, behind much older girls, at the U.S. senior championship.

It was 1994, though, that Michelle made her first really big national splash. Several days before the U.S. Figure Skating Championships began, two thugs attacked favorite Nancy Kerrigan. She could not compete. While Nancy watched from a box seat, her rival, Tonya Harding, took the U.S. title. Michelle, who was just 13 and weighed less than 80 pounds, finished second. Normally, the second-place finisher goes to the Olympics. But officials may place top skaters who were injured during nationals onto the team. Nancy was put on the team. She was favored to win the gold medal.

Michelle went to the Olympics as an alternate but did not compete. She finished eighth at the world championships! In 1995, Michelle place fourth at the worlds. Yet, some international skating officials complained that she still looked like a young junior skater. Michelle *did* look like a little girl. She wore her hair in a ponytail and wore no makeup on the ice.

After that, Coach Carroll talked her parents into letting her have a more mature look. At the 1996 world championships, Michelle looked 10 years older! She wore eye makeup and a braided bun and costumes like the older women. She skated as they did too. In fact, she skated better! Michelle won her first world championship at age 15. Through 2000, Michelle had been first or second in the world four years in a row.

And her brother doesn't even play hockey anymore!

DIVES

PAT McCORMICK
AND
LAURA WILKINSON

*T*he 10-meter diving platform is 33 feet in the air. Diving from it is like jumping from a three-story building. Sound scary? Not to Pat McCormick and Laura Wilkinson. They were both brave enough to somersault and twist their way off the platform to Olympic gold medals. Their courage came in handy, too: Pat had to battle attitudes against married moms participating in sports, and Laura dived through the pain of a broken foot.

PAT
McCORMICK

WHEN PATRICIA MCCORMICK WAS A KID, LITTLE GIRLS WERE expected to play dolls, not sports. When they grew up, they were expected to become full-time housewives and mothers. But Pat always wanted something else — and she got it.

At the 1952 Olympics, in Helsinki, Finland, Pat won gold medals in three-meter springboard *and* 10-meter platform diving. At the time, only three divers had ever done that (another three did it after Pat).

In 1956, the graceful athlete swept both diving events

again, at the Melbourne (Australia) Olympics. *No* other diver had accomplished that double-double, and only one has done it since. (Greg Louganis of the U.S. swept the men's events in 1984 and 1988.)

Oh, and along the way, Pat *had* become a house-wife and mother, just as she was "supposed" to do!

Growing up in Southern California during the 1930's and '40s, young Pat Keller participated in several individual sports (Team sports for girls were rare). She participated in swimming, diving, and golf. When Pat was 14, someone saw her dive and invited her to the Los Angeles Athletic Club.

The great divers there inspired Pat. She told her mother she wanted to become an Olympic diving champion. Pat's mom supported her goal. Mrs.

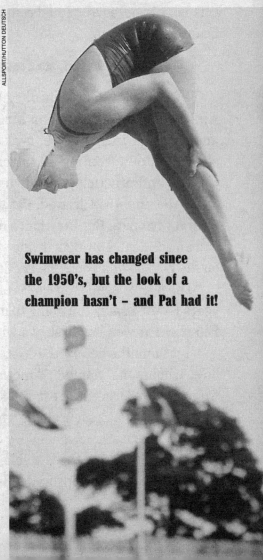

ALLSPORT/HUTTON DEUTSCH

Swimwear has changed since the 1950's, but the look of a champion hasn't – and Pat had it!

Keller would earn money telling fortunes by reading tea leaves to help pay Pat's trolley fare to the Club for lessons.

In 1948, at age 18, Pat went to the Olympic trials and missed making the team by one hundredth of a point. She was not discouraged. "I had come so close, I realized I could beat them," she said.

TRAIN, TRAIN, TRAIN

That year Pat met someone else who thought she could win: swimming coach Glenn McCormick. They fell in love and married in 1949. Glenn also became her coach. Pat settled into a routine of attending Long Beach City College and practicing her diving — six hours a day!

By the time 1952 arrived, Pat was in top shape and ready for the Olympics. But less than a month before the trials, she had an accident. During a diving show, she cut open her head on the bottom of a pool. She needed 50 stitches.

"The doctor said, 'You can't compete,' " she remembered years later. "I said, 'I'm going to make the team.' And I did!" Did she! Pat won her first two Olympic gold medals.

Eight months before the 1956 Olympics, Pat had a baby boy, whom she named Timothy. Back then, pregnant women were urged to rest a lot and not do anything too physical. But Pat kept training until four months before the baby was born. She swam every day until he was born and was back in training three weeks later.

Many people disapproved. "In the fifties, women just

didn't have a child and get back into competing," Pat said. "I could hardly find a doctor who would work with me." Pat's family *was* supportive. Most days, she stayed with the baby in the morning and her mother or mother-in-law would watch him while she trained, often until 10 at night.

Pat qualified for the Olympics and won the springboard competition at Melbourne by a comfortable margin to pocket her third gold medal. But the platform diving event was more difficult. With only two dives remaining, Pat found herself in fourth place. "It got down to the last dive, and it had to be the dive of my life to win," Pat remembered.

It was! Pat did a full twisting 1 ½ somersault so well that it earned her some perfect scores. She beat U.S. teammates Juno Irwin-Stover and Paula Jean Meyers to complete her amazing double-double.

A DIVING DAUGHTER

Pat retired from competitive diving after the Olympics. She did some commercial endorsements for sports products and bore another child, a daughter she named Kelly. The McCormicks didn't push their kids to dive, but Kelly chose to take up the sport. In 1984, 28 years after her mother completed her feat, Kelly McCormick won a silver medal in springboard diving at the Los Angeles Olympics. She won a bronze four years later, in Seoul, South Korea.

No one was prouder of Kelly than her mom, the high-diving housewife named Patricia Keller McCormick. ♔

LAURA WILKINSON

LAURA WILKINSON DIDN'T HAVE TO OVERCOME SEXISM OR racism or poverty to become a diving champion. All she had to deal with was history, low expectations, and a broken foot!

Laura unexpectedly became one of the biggest American heroes of the 2000 Olympics, when she won the gold medal in 10-meter platform diving. She was the first U.S. woman to win that event in *36 years*. The way Laura won made it even more exciting: She rallied from eighth place to win — and she did it despite three broken bones in her right foot!

People watching on TV felt goose bumps during Laura's last two dives. The other divers looked tense before their takeoffs. Laura limped up the steps to the platform and smiled at everyone who was cheering. She was confident! Sure enough, she defeated China's Li Na by 1.74 points

A LONG SHOT

Laura was a long shot to win the gold medal even before she broke her foot. The Chinese had dominated diving for 20 years, winning four straight Olympic gold medals and three of the last four world platform titles. The U.S. women hadn't won a single diving medal at the 1996 Olympics and only one at the 1992 Games. Laura had won only one major international title in her life, the 1998 Goodwill Games.

But Laura could dream, couldn't she? Yes, but her dream of winning an Olympic medal seemed to be over six months before the 2000 Games, when she broke her foot. She was practicing her inward 2½ somersault during dry-land training. She hit her right foot on a wooden platform and landed hard on a floor mat. Three bones broke.

The next morning at 6 A.M., her coach, Ken Armstrong, pounded on Laura's door. When she answered, he said, "We worked a long time for this moment. I don't care if they cut your leg off, you're going to make this team."

Instead of operating, doctors put Laura's foot in a cast so that she could practice.

Laura became the first U.S. woman in 36 years to win Olympic gold in platform diving.

Well, sort of. For two months, she practiced her approach to the dives, hopping on one foot. Then she visualized, or imagined, doing them. After the cast came off, she practiced dives underwater.

About six weeks before the Olympic trials, Laura finally was allowed to start practicing real dives. It was difficult and very painful. She couldn't run

MANNY MILLAN/SPORTS ILLUSTRATED

on her foot, so she couldn't compete on springboard or do forward dives, because they require running approaches. She could barely walk up the steps to the platform.

Laura placed first in the Olympic trials, anyway, and was on her way! In the preliminaries at Sydney, she missed her inward 2½ somersault and finished fifth. She missed that dive again in the semifinals and fell to eighth place.

But that night, in the finals, Laura hit the first two of her dives and moved up to fifth place. Then came a reverse 2½ somersault in the tuck position. "I went all out on the third dive," Laura said. "I didn't hold anything back."

The judges noticed! She got 9's and 9.5's (out of 10). Then the four women ahead of her all did poor dives and Laura was in first place! Next came that troublesome inward 2½ in the pike position. The setup hurt Laura's foot, and she always feared she was going to hit the platform on the dive. It wasn't perfect, but the dive was good enough to hold the lead after the other four divers performed.

Laura's last dive was an inward 2½ somersault with a half-twist. She nailed it, collecting a bunch of 8.0's, 8.5's, and 9.0's. When Laura realized she had won the gold medal, she grabbed her coach in a big hug.

Later, Laura told reporters how much she loved comeback stories. She had read lots of inspirational stories to cheer herself up when her foot was in a cast.

"If I could be an inspiration to someone else, that would be a dream come true," she said. It was.

KICKS

MICHELLE AKERS AND BRANDI CHASTAIN

Many people believe women's sports finally came of age when the U.S. team won the World Cup. That team did something men hadn't been able to do: make soccer popular in the United States. The sport's history in the U.S. isn't long enough to have a true "then" hero, but we've paired one of the women's team's original stars, Michelle Akers, with the woman whose heroics symbolize the triumph of women's sports, Brandi Chastain.

MICHELLE AKERS

ON AUGUST 21, 1985, MICHELLE AKERS SCORED THE VERY first goal in the history of the U.S. Women's Soccer Team. Fourteen years later, when the U.S. team won the Women's World Cup on a thrilling shoot-out in Pasadena, California, the curly-topped, super-competitive star was there, too. She stood — battered and bruised, having leapt up from a stretcher in the training room — on the winners' podium with her teammates.

When it comes to U.S. women's soccer, Michelle was *always* there. She had been a member of the first U.S.

Neither opponents nor injuries and illness could stop Michelle from being a star.

women's soccer team when it was formed at the U.S. Olympic Festival at Baton Rouge, Louisiana, in 1985.

Long before Mia Hamm, Michelle was the team's greatest star, with a knack for scoring that devastated opponents and a shot that was so hard it was compared to a cannon blast. She led the team to the first Women's World Cup title ever, in 1991, and helped it capture the first women's Olympic gold medal, in 1996. As a striker and, later, as a midfielder, Michelle scored key goal after key goal, and retired in 2000 as the team's second all-time leading scorer.

Michelle had planned to play in the 2000 Olympics, in Sydney, Australia, too. But, she retired a month before the

Summer Games because of a shoulder injury and her long-time struggle with an illness called Chronic Fatigue Syndrome, or CFS. With CFS, a person is extremely tired all the time. She also suffers from migraine headaches, sleeplessness, and, in Michelle's case, high blood pressure.

It was difficult for Michelle to retire. She is *very* tough and had never allowed her CFS or injuries to slow her down. She had 13 knee operations during her career. After she got CFS, she rested as much as possible between games so that she could play as many minutes as her team needed.

NOW, THAT'S TOUGH

Here's an example of how tough she is: During the final game of the 1999 Women's World Cup, against China, Michelle was knocked unconscious while trying to head-block a corner kick. The U.S. goalkeeper, Brianna Scurry, accidentally punched her in the head. When Michelle woke up, she was in a room in the stadium with IV tubes in her arms and an oxygen mask on her face. On a nearby TV, she could see her teammates were in the midst of a shoot-out. When they won, Michelle insisted on taking the needles out of her arms and staggered out to join her team!

The U.S. team missed Michelle in Sydney. Some fans say the team wouldn't have lost the gold medal to Norway if she had played. Michelle watched the game from a box seat at the stadium and cried when her team lost.

Michelle was born February 1, 1966, and grew up in

Seattle, Washington. People called her a tomboy because they saw her playing football with the boys of the neighborhood. But no one tried to stop Michelle, perhaps because Title IX had already begun to change people's attitudes toward girls and sports. (Title IX, part of a federal law that was passed in 1972, requires girls be given the same athletic opportunities as boys.)

Michelle's younger brother, Michael, played soccer, and Michelle loved sports, so her mother signed her up for soccer when she was 8. Michelle didn't like it at first and wanted to quit. The worst part was the uniforms: pink and yellow, what she called "girlie colors." But she stayed with it, and soon soccer became an important part of her life.

CAUSING TROUBLE

When Michelle was 11, her parents divorced. Her father moved a few blocks away. Michelle and Michael saw him every Thursday night and every other weekend. The only time they saw their parents together was at their soccer games. Their mom and dad sat at opposite ends of the sideline. After the games, though, they would come together to talk to Michael or Michelle about his or her game.

Soccer became Michelle's best friend. She has said that she was confused and rebelled. She skipped school, dated older guys, even experimented with drugs. But her soccer coach, Mr. Kovaks, helped her change. She became a Christian like him, and that turned her life around.

Thanks in part to Title IX, Michelle received a scholarship to play soccer at the University of Central Florida. She graduated with a degree in liberal studies and health.

In 1985, Michelle became a member of the first U.S. women's soccer team. She was just a sophomore in college. You might say that she and the team grew up together. (You also might say that women's sports in general have grown up with the soccer team because the team helped gain acceptance for female athletes.)

When Michelle was a little girl, she wore a Pittsburgh Steelers' jersey because she was a big fan of the pro football team. In fact, she dreamed of being a wide receiver for the Steelers. By the mid-1990's, lots of little girls were wearing *Michelle's* jersey. She and the women's team had given girls sports heroes whom they could actually imitate.

Michelle takes her position as a role model seriously and always goes out of her way to be nice to her fans. She speaks to youth groups often, and she has a website (www.michelleakers.com). Kids can learn more about Michelle and e-mail her there

Once, a little girl knocked on Michelle's door and asked her to come out and kick soccer balls with her and her friends. Michelle did just that. She also brought out pictures, books, and pins for all the kids.

Michelle knows you can be tough *and* nice. That's a model any athlete should follow.

BRANDI CHASTAIN

With one very well-placed, left-footed kick in July 1999, Brandi Chastain became the most famous female soccer player in the world.

Of course, it wasn't just *any* kick. It was the penalty kick that gave the U.S. women's soccer team its dramatic shootout victory over China in the 1999 World Cup. More than 90,000 fans were watching Brandi at the crowded Rose Bowl, in Pasadena, California. Millions more were watching on TV. The fact that Brandi used her off-foot (the weaker one) to get the ball by Chinese goalkeeper Gao Hong made the kick especially impressive. Many players can't make a penalty kick with their off-foot, but Brandi had been practicing left-footed shots. She was ready.

After the ball went in, Brandi did something that burned the moment of victory into the memory of every person who saw her. She ripped off her shirt, fell to her knees, and thrust her arms into the air in victory. Brandi's face glowed with joy, and dozens of photographers caught the moment.

The picture of Brandi was used in newspapers all over the world. It also appeared on the cover of *Time*, *Newsweek*, and *Sports Illustrated*. Brandi was an instant celebrity. She was invited to appear on the television show *Late Night with David Letterman*. Her portrait appeared on boxes of Wheaties. The famous photograph also caused discussion because some people thought she should not have taken off her shirt (She had on a sports bra, which is like the top of a two-piece bathing suit.)

In a way, the photo was a great symbol of the progress women's sports have made. Girls and women have been fighting for decades to prove that they have as much right to play sports as boys and men — and that they can do it without being any less feminine. During the World Cup, many sports fans saw that progress for the first time. They realized that Brandi and her teammates were athletic *and* also feminine.

It was fitting that Brandi became the focus of attention, because she is outgoing and talkative. "She always wanted the chance to be a voice for the sport," said her World Cup coach, Tony DiCicco. "She just needed that one kick to do it."

JOHN W. McDONOUGH/SPORTS ILLUSTRATED

After Brandi won the Cup with her famous goal, she shed her shirt joyfully – and got people talking!

Brandi had to overcome many challenges to reach the top of her sport. She started playing soccer when she was 8 years old and entered the University of California on an athletic scholarship in 1986. She injured both knees badly, had surgery on both legs, and didn't play college soccer for two years. She transferred to Santa Clara University. The team became a national power and made it to the national semi-finals Brandi's junior and senior years.

ON THE TEAM, AND OFF

In 1988, Brandi was named to the U.S. national soccer team. She was a substitute forward, but she tried to make the most of her opportunities. During qualifying for the first-ever Women's World Cup, in 1991, she came off the bench to score five straight goals in a 12–0 win over Mexico. She finished the qualifying tournament with seven goals. At the World Cup finals, Brandi played in two games and started one to help the U.S. win the championship.

Brandi played little for the national team in 1992, and not at all in 1993, 1994 and the first eight months of 1995. For two of those years, she was playing pro soccer in Japan. She was even named her team's Most Valuable Player in 1993.

In September 1995, U.S. soccer officials asked Brandi to return to the national team. They wanted her to become a defender, though. Brandi had been a forward since she was a little girl. Changing positions wasn't easy. But Brandi is a great student of the game. She studied the position, and she worked hard. When the team played Russia at a tournament in Brazil in January 1996, Brandi started at defender.

By the time the U.S. team arrived at the 1996 Olympics, in Atlanta, Georgia, Brandi had become a key member of the team. She played every minute of every U.S. game. She played the gold-medal game in pain because she had hurt a knee badly in the 2–1 semifinal victory against Norway.

Americans became more interested in women's team sports during the 1996 Olympics. That interest reached new levels in 1999 when the Women's World Cup was played in the United States for the first time. Record crowds attended games all around the country. Few people were focusing on Brandi. Mia Hamm, Michelle Akers, and Briana Scurry were the stars. Brandi got some attention after a quarterfinal match against Germany: She accidentally scored for the other team! She felt bad and, in the second half, scored a goal that tied the game, 2–2.

It was that mental strength that earned Brandi a chance to make the Cup-winning kick. When Coach DiCicco asked assistant coach Lauren Gregg to make a lineup for the penalty kick shoot-off, Brandi was not included. She had missed a penalty shot in an exhibition loss to China four months earlier. But Coach DiCicco didn't feel right about leaving such a steady, confident player off the list. He walked over to Brandi and asked, "Do you think you can make it?"

"Yeah, I do," Brandi said.

She was right.

TRACK

JACKIE JOYNER-KERSEE AND MARION JONES

One of these athletes won five Olympic medals at one Games; the other one has six medals, won at four Olympics. One was named the Greatest Female Athlete of the 20th Century; the other has been called the greatest female athlete of the future. They are Jackie Joyner-Kersee and Marion Jones, two track wonder women.

JACKIE JOYNER-KERSEE

SOMEDAY, WHEN THE PEOPLE IN CHARGE OF SELECTING THE greatest athletes who ever lived are meeting, the name Jackie Joyner-Kersee will be placed at the top of many lists. In 2000, actually, Jackie was named the Greatest Female Athlete of the 20th Century by *Sports Illustrated for Women*, not just for her athletic accomplishments but for what she meant to women's sports in general.

Indeed. With amazing grace and terrific power, Jackie was the first woman of track and field for nearly 15 years. She won a total of six medals, three of them gold, in four Olympics from 1984 to 1996. She set four world records in the heptathlon — a grueling seven-event competition which tests speed, strength, coordination, and almost every other athletic skill. She also played college and pro basketball. "You saw her and you got the idea of what a woman athlete should be," soccer star Mia Hamm told *SI For Women*.

When Jackie was born, in 1962, her grandmother said she would be the first lady of something. That's why, the famous story goes, she was named after the nation's first lady, Jackie Kennedy. Jackie was the second-oldest of four children. The oldest was her brother Al, who won an Olympic bronze medal in the long jump in 1984 and later married another track star, the late Florence Griffith-Joyner ("Flo-Jo"). Jackie would someday marry an athlete and coach, Bobby Kersee.

So, according to *Sports Illustrated*, Jackie "was shaped by a mother who bound her to excellence;

STEVEN E. SUTTON/DUOMO

The javelin was one of seven events Jackie competed in over two days in the grueling heptathlon.

by an older brother who was an admirer, defender, and soul mate; and by a coach who demanded the best use of her gifts and did it so selflessly that she eventually married him."

FAMILY TIES

Jackie's parents, Alfred and Mary, were in their mid-teens when she was born, and didn't have much money. There was plenty of love and discipline in the house, but outside, things were much different. The Joyners lived in a violent neighborhood where street shootings were common. When she was only 11, Jackie saw a man gunned down right in front of her house!

Jackie was lucky, though, because she had a strong family and much encouragement at school and in sports. When she was 12, she saw a movie on TV about Babe Didrickson Zaharias. Babe had been an amazing athlete who excelled at every sport she tried. She won three gold medals in track and field at the 1932 Olympics and 31 pro golf championships. She was an AAU All-America in basketball and a standout in softball. Babe could do anything! Jackie decided she wanted to be just like Babe. And she had at least one coach who believed she could do that.

Jackie's mother was very strict and did not allow Jackie to date until she was 18. So Jackie concentrated on her schoolwork and on athletics. When she graduated, in 1980, Jackie was in the top ten percent of her class at Lincoln High School. Jackie also had been offered athletic scholarships to UCLA in both basketball and track and field. Believe it or not, she grabbed the basketball offer.

Jackie was at college for only a few months when tragedy struck. Her mother developed deadly meningitis and died, at age 37. Jackie was only 18.

After she returned to school, Jackie was drawn to Bob Kersee, an assistant track coach. Bob, too, lost his mother very young, so that he knew from experience what Jackie was going through. He also encouraged her to excel in every way.

Taking on the heptathlon certainly gave Jackie an opportunity to do that. Heptathletes compete in the high jump, 100-meter hurdles, shot put, and 200-meter run in one day, and in the long jump, javelin throw, and 800-meter run the next day. They earn points in each event, and the athlete with the most points wins.

GATHERING GOLD

At the 1984 Olympics, in Los Angeles, California, Jackie won a silver medal in the heptathlon. In 1986 — the year Jackie and Bob were married — she broke the 7,000-point level in the event. The heptathlon was Jackie's event, and she wanted to own it.

Over the next few years, she did. At the 1988 Olympics, she set a world record of 7,291 points to win the heptathlon gold. She also won a gold medal for the long jump there. At the 1992 Games, Jackie defended her heptathlon title and won bronze in the long jump. Her final Olympic performance came in 1996, in Atlanta, Georgia. Although she hurt herself so badly in the heptathlon preliminaries that she had to withdraw, she leaped through the pain to one last medal, a bronze in the long jump.

Jackie has had other opponents to deal with besides her competitors on the field. She suffers from severe asthma. In 1993, in Stuttgart, Germany, she won the heptathlon world championship, but suffered one of the worst asthma attacks of her life. During the 1995 USA championships, she had to wear a mask while competing to avoid the pollen that could trigger her allergies.

In 1998, Jackie retired from track and field competition, but she is active in other things. She heads the St. Louis Sports Commission. She and Bob put together a NASCAR team, JKR Motorsports, to compete in stock-car races across the country. She is also a spokeswoman in the battle against crippling asthma and has several business interests.

Perhaps the activity closest to Jackie's heart, though, is her efforts to help the kids in her old East St. Louis neighborhood. When she was growing up, Jackie spent a lot of time at the Mary E. Brown Community Center. There she met her friends, did homework, and played sports. Later, the Center was neglected badly. Jackie's goal is to get it back on its feet, for other neighborhood kids to enjoy.

Didn't we say, Jackie Joyner-Kersee is the greatest?

At the 2000 Olympics,
Marion won the 100
and 200 meters –
and five medals!

AL TIELEMANS/SPORTS ILLUSTRATED

MARION JONES

Jackie Joyner-Kersee may have retired just in time. If she had not stepped aside as track-and-field's superwoman, Marion Jones might have pushed her! Marion was called the greatest sprint talent ever while she was in high school. At the 2000 Summer Olympics, "the fastest woman in the world" set a record for most medals won by a female athlete at one Olympics. Marion won five medals: three gold and two bronze. She also became the first woman in 12 years to take home three track-and-field gold medals from one Olympic Games.

How did Marion get so good so fast? Desire, hard work, and strong family support had *something* to do with it.

A FIRM FOUNDATION

Marion was raised by her mother, Marion Toler, who was a single parent from the Central American nation of Belize. Ms. Toler worked hard, sometimes holding several jobs at one time, to support her family. Education was the most important thing to her, but she also wanted Marion and her brother, Albert, to have sports opportunities.

Albert is five years older than Marion. She loved to be included in his activities. "I would constantly run around with his friends," Marion recalled. "I had to run a little faster than kids my age to stay up with them."

She always had her eye on the goal of Olympic gold. When she was 7 or 8, Marion wrote on the chalkboard of her bedroom: THE '92 OLYMPICS IN BARCELONA. "I wasn't really involved in track and field at that time," Marion said, years later. "I was involved in other sports: tee-ball, baseball, gymnastics, and tap dancing. But I knew I wanted to be successful in some type of athletic endeavor, and that was the ultimate goal: the Olympics."

In life, as on the track, Marion got off to a quick start. As a freshman at Rio Mesa High School, in Oxnard, California, she ran the 100 meters in 11.62 and the 200 in 23.70. She became the first freshman ever to win California state titles in both events. When she was a junior, she improved her times to 11.17 and 22.58 and qualified for the track-and-field trials for the 1992 Olympics. Marion placed fifth in the 100 meters and fourth in the 200 meters. Her time in the 200 earned her a place as an alternate on the relay team. marion's dream of Barcelona in 1992 had come true! But didn't go. "I didn't want to rush things," she said.

Marion was just as good at basketball as track. As a senior, she averaged 22.8 points and 14.7 rebounds and was named California Division I player of the year. She earned a basketball scholarship to the University of North Carolina (UNC).

During her freshman year at UNC, Marion broke into the starting lineup after only four games. She scored an average of 14.2 points per game and helped UNC win the NCAA Championship. The next season, Marion became the first female player in UNC history to score 1,000 points by her sophomore season.

CHOOSING ONE SPORT

Marion stepped right up in track, too. As a freshman, she earned All-America honors in four events: the long jump, the 100 meters, the 200 meters, and the 4 x 100-meter relay.

In order to excel on a world-class level, Marion learned she might have to concentrate on one sport. After she broke a bone in her foot playing basketball in summer 1995, she decided to sit out the 1995-96 basketball season to train for the Olympic track trials. But she hurt her foot again in December 1995 and couldn't compete at all.

Marion trained hard to recover from her injury, but she also found time for other things. In 1998, she graduated from college and married C.J. Hunter, a fellow student-athlete at UNC and a world-class shot-putter.

The next two years were spent preparing for the 2000 Olympics. Marion battled some minor injuries but kept on going, training five hours a day, six days a week most of the time. "I can't be satisfied unless I know I'm training harder than anybody else in the world," she said.

After Marion qualified for the 2000 Olympics in five events, she made a stunning prediction: she would win *five* gold medals at the Games. The prediction became the buzz leading up to the Olympics. Could she do it? Would she go home a partial winner, or empty-handed?

On September 23, 2000, Marion won with the 100-meter dash easily. Then she took the gold in 200. Marion knew that the long jump would be the hardest event for her. Sure enough, she came away with only (!) a bronze. She went on to collect two more medals: a bronze in the 4 x 100 relay and a gold in the 4 x 40.

Still, in winning five track-and-field medals, Marion did something no other woman had ever done. And she was only 24 years old. The best may be yet to come.